THE HAUNTING OF JIM CROW

Allan Havis

BROADWAY PLAY PUBLISHING INC
New York
www.broadwayplaypublishing.com
info@broadwayplaypublishing.com

THE HAUNTING OF JIM CROW
© Copyright 2005 by Allan Havis

cover image by Maryann Callery

First printing: December 2005
I S B N: 978-0-88145-278-5

Book design: Marie Donovan
Word processing: Microsoft Word
Typographic controls: Xerox Ventura Publisher 2.0 P E
Typeface: Palatino
Printed and bound in the U S A

Commissioned by Thurgood Marshall College/
University of California, San Diego and presented
originally as a radio production on K P B S, F M,
San Diego 17 May 2004

LEZA .... Sylvia M'Lafi Thompson
SENATOR THURMOND ....Dale Morris
ESSIE MAE WASHINGTON-WILLIAMS .....Brooke Battle
EARL WARREN, LYNDON JOHNSON,
ROBERT KENNEDY .... Craig Huisenga
HUGO BLACK, JAMES EASTLAND .... Dick Emmet
THURGOOD MARSHALL .... Anthony Drummond
CARL MURPHY .... Laurence Brown
VOICE OF LORETTA .... Leigh Anne Bradstreet

Director .... Delicia Turner Sonnenberg
Stage manager .... Leigh Anne Bradstreet
Set & costume design .... Jennifer Brawn Gittings
Light design .... Maria Bane Jacobs
Sound design .... Rachel Le Vine

CHARACTERS & SETTING

LEZA, *mixed race, late fifties, high school teacher*

SENATOR STROM THURMOND, *junior Senator from South Carolina*

ESSIE MAE WASHINGTON-WILLIAMS, THURMOND'S *mixed race daughter*

EARL WARREN, *new Supreme Court Chief Justice*

HUGO BLACK, WARREN'S *colleague on the Supreme Court*

THURGOOD MARSHALL, *N A A C P chief attorney*

CARL MURPHY, *publisher of a leading black publication*

and the off stage voices of:
LYNDON JOHNSON, *U S President*
ROBERT KENNEDY, *New York Senator*
JAMES EASTLAND, *Mississippi Senator/Judiciary Chairman*
LORETTA, THURMOND'S *secretary*

Los Angeles, 2004,

Washington D C, 1955, 1960, 1964, 1967, 2002

Little Rock, Arkansas, 1957

SPECIAL THANKS

To Cecil Lytle, Michael Schudson, Abraham Shragge, Ginnah Saunders, Sandra Stanton, Lance Rogers, Maryann Callery, Angela Carone and her staff at K P B S radio, San Diego Museum of Contemporary Arts, and most especially, Thurgood Marshall College at U C San Diego.

to my darling wife Julia

PROLOGUE

(February 2005. A Slightly decrepid classroom in South Central, Los Angeles)

LEZA: *(Warm, but with a sardonic edge)* The last time this room was painted was fifteen years ago. Welcome to my classroom. *(Pause)* My name is Leza. My last name is unimportant. I teach high school social studies in South Central. It's not easy work and the neighborhood is terribly poor. I hope to retire soon despite a modest pension. *(Pause)* Two Decembers ago I was astonished by a public announcement made at the Adam's Mark Hotel in Columbia, South Carolina. Seventy nine year old Essie Mae Washington-Williams told the world that her father's name is James Strom Thurmond and in her words, "at last I feel completely free." *(Pause)* Essie Mae was my teacher many years ago. Her autobiography just came out last month. She had great energy, warmth, and enthusiasm. She gave me direction in life. I have no idea how she was able to maintain her silence about Senator Strom Thurmond—the oldest Senator in American history. Clearly, she loved him enough to wait until his death, June 23, 2003. I assume it was love. What else could it be? *(Pause)* I tell my classes this piece of news about Essie Mae and Strom for a variety of reasons. I also remind them about what is probably the biggest decision by the Supreme Court in the last century—1954 Brown v. Board of Education. Most of this history just goes over their heads or down the nearest toilet. *(Pause)* My kids in class never heard the name Jim Crow, never heard of Jim Crow laws, or Jim Crow schools. *(Pause)* Thurgood Marshall on behalf of

the N A A C P argued for integration in every public
school in America. Marshall won clearly in the Supreme
Court, but many think it was a Pyrrhic victory. *(Pause)*
In March 1956, Strom Thurmond led many of his
Senate colleagues to initiate a Southern Manifesto
in protest to the Supreme Court's "social activism.
This congressional rebellion helped to ignite racist
mobs in all too many communities. *(Pause)* I think back
to the school days with my teacher Essie Mae Williams-
Washington. I have so many questions to ask her today.
Like Essie Mae, I also have black and white family.
And I would give anything to go back fifty years with
her. She was in the unique position to see two separate
societies spinning like two heads of a coin. *(Pause)*
Two heads of a coin. Senator Strom Thurmond
and Justice Thurgood Marshall. Two pronounced
individuals on opposite sides destined for scandal
and fame. Destined to meet in a most public way.
(Pause) Essie Mae was the first child of an American
icon who lived and worked in the Senate longer than
any one. With my eyes closed, I imagine I am holding
Essie Mae's gentle, outstretched hand. *(Pause)* And in
1955, Essie Mae makes her arduous visit from rural
Pennsylvania to the nation's capital to see her father,
Senator Strom Thurmond. I truly wonder how these
two manage their personal affairs.

(Pause)

Imagine. April 1955, Washington, DC.

Scene One

(SENATOR THURMOND's *office, Washington D C. April
1955*)

SENATOR: *(On the phone)* I distinctly recall asking for the
master barber to come to my office, Loretta! *(Pause)* Not

tomorrow, today. Five minutes ago. *(Pause)* Now darling, I did certainly request ol' Marvin, the chubby colored barber from Dupont Circle. So get him please in a pre-paid livery and within the hour, God help you, or I'll take away your sweet little Christmas gift. Thank you so much, sweet Loretta. *(Hangs up and lights a cigarette. To himself)* And goddamn it we're out of cigarettes and candy mints. *(Busies himself with papers and his intercom buzzes)* Yes?

INTERCOM: Essie Mae Williams is here.

SENATOR: Does she have an appointment?

INTERCOM: Yes.

SENATOR: It's really not a convenient time.

INTERCOM: Shall I send her away or have her wait?

SENATOR: Loretta, don't forget to phone Lyndon Johnson before quitting time.

INTERCOM: Yes, sir.

SENATOR: Send her in, but buzz me with a "crisis" in five minutes.

INTERCOM: Of course, Senator.

SENATOR: I'm just kidding.

(The SENATOR *rocks back in his seat. In a moment* ESSIE MAE WASHINGTON *enters.)*

SENATOR: Good afternoon, Essie Mae. Is it raining?

ESSIE MAE: Yes.

SENATOR: Please. Have a seat.

ESSIE MAE: Thank you.

SENATOR: Would you like a hand towel?

ESSIE MAE: No.

SENATOR: You look much older and so elegant. Is that a new hat?

ESSIE MAE: Yes, Senator.

SENATOR: I so love women's hats, Essie Mae. I think that is the secret behind the beauty of refined, southern ladies.

ESSIE MAE: It helps ward off the rain.

SENATOR: A good hat distracts my eye from a lady's shapely leg. A cigarette?

ESSIE MAE: No thank you. I gave it up.

SENATOR: *(Charming tease)* South Carolina is a tobacco state. You have to help our economy. Would you like coffee or a coca cola?

ESSIE MAE: Coca Cola would be nice.

SENATOR: *(Buzzes. On intercom)* A tall Coca Cola with ice and a gentle twist of lemon. And a hand towel. Thank you, Loretta *(Pause)* Your dear mother never wore a hat. She liked scarves. Beautiful red scarves. And I always told her that red was a beautiful color in the morning sun. She never liked compliments which made me so god-awful tongue tied. How long are you in Washington?

ESSIE MAE: A few days.

SENATOR: Splendid.

ESSIE MAE: It's a fascinating city.

SENATOR: Indeed it is.

ESSIE MAE: You have new staff.

SENATOR: Yes. I'm a bigger man now.

ESSIE MAE: They don't know me.

SENATOR: Well, they are quite new. Give them time. They know how to be discreet. How is your job?

ESSIE MAE: I love teaching.

SENATOR: I envy you. You look sad.

ESSIE MAE: I'm sorry.

SENATOR: How can I help, my dear?

ESSIE MAE: I remember our first meeting back in Edgefield.

SENATOR: Of course, your mother was quite sick then.

ESSIE MAE: She took me by the hand to your law office. I was sixteen.

SENATOR: You were the picture of absolute beauty and youth. I have a photograph of you from that visit.

ESSIE MAE: Do you?

SENATOR: I keep it in my home study. Much safer there. I have a few photographs too of your last years at South Carolina State. Exquisite photographs of graduation. I hope you keep my photographs within proper reach.

ESSIE MAE: You know my aunt is very ill in Coatesville.

SENATOR: Yes, so you wrote. You have several aunts in Pennsylvania.

ESSIE MAE: I think she needs an operation.

SENATOR: Oh dear Jesus...

ESSIE MAE: Whatever you can do would be a godsend.

SENATOR: Do you need money?

ESSIE MAE: I thought you could call her this week.

SENATOR: Of course. Just give my secretary the phone number.

ESSIE MAE: Thank you.

SENATOR: Good diet is crucial for long health. And exercise! Walking, running, jumping, swimming, each and every day including Sunday, Essie Mae. You know what makes me so unique in all of Washington?

ESSIE MAE: You're the stingiest tipper in the Senate.

(The SENATOR *laughs warmly.)*

ESSIE MAE: You exercise more than any other man in the Senate.

SENATOR: That's right, little angel. But there's another reason why I stand out.

ESSIE MAE: You're the first Senator to reach office as a write-in candidate.

SENATOR: And I'm very proud of it! I am the people's legitimate choice. Voters had to write out my full and complete name on a ballot. *(Pause)* How is your husband Julius?

ESSIE MAE: Fine.

SENATOR: Please convey my respects to him.

ESSIE MAE: I will.

SENATOR: He's an exceptional lawyer.

ESSIE MAE: Yes, he is.

SENATOR: He's keen on the new Supreme Court, isn't he?

ESSIE MAE: I suppose.

SENATOR: Brown v. Board of Education.

ESSIE MAE: It's on his mind, naturally.

SENATOR: Ticking time bomb, Essie Mae. Tears my heart in two.

ESSIE MAE: How do you think the court will decide?

SENATOR: The country moves like a glacier. The court should be mindful of the pained soul of this country.

ESSIE MAE: Not every colored child has a benefactor.

SENATOR: I do realize that.

ESSIE MAE: Do you?

SENATOR: We're all burdened by Jim Crow laws, but this need not be an American tragedy.

ESSIE MAE: Children can mix freely. The younger the easier it would be. Believe me...as a teacher I know.

SENATOR: And that is God's great wish?

ESSIE MAE: Yes.

SENATOR: Then God needs to address each southern state in due time. *(Checks his watch)*

ESSIE MAE: In due time, sir. *(Pause)* You work too much.

SENATOR: Yes, my dear.

ESSIE MAE: You should pay more attention to your wife.

SENATOR: Well, I probably should. Jean is a much younger woman and it's hard to catch her each weekend.

ESSIE MAE: I worry for you.

SENATOR: Very kind of you to say so.

(Intercom buzzes. He picks up the phone.)

SENATOR: Yes? *(Pause, he frowns.)* Now? All right Loretta. I can put out that fire. Give me one moment. *(Hangs up. Smiles)* Won't you please stay for lunch?

ESSIE MAE: That would be nice. Perhaps another time.

SENATOR: Thank you, Essie Mae. You know, when my office door is closed, I don't expect a handshake. Is that too much to ask?

* * *

LEZA: Chief Justice Earl Warren is having lunch with Justice Hugo Black. Where much of the high court business is on the menu of the day.

Scene Two

(Washington D C. Late afternoon. Upscale restaurant. Chief Justice EARL WARREN *is having lunch with Justice* HUGO BLACK.*)*

WARREN: You haven't touched you plate, Hugo.

BLACK: Heartburn. Maybe an ulcer.

WARREN: I'm picking up the check. Order something else.

BLACK: I'll just drink, Earl.

WARREN: Nonsense. Have an omelet. That's quite gentle on the tummy.

BLACK: You sound like a radio ad.

WARREN: Thank you.

BLACK: I should stay in Alabama. I'm tired of this town.

WARREN: You sound like a broken record.

BLACK: So?

WARREN: *(Gentle humor)* You can fish and hunt all you want here.

BLACK: Is that right?

WARREN: Would a justice lie to another justice?

BLACK: Yes, all the time.

WARREN: I miss the west coast.

BLACK: Then complain to Eisenhower and I'll complain to F D R.

WARREN: It's easy to vent to a corpse, my friend. A ghost simply taps back on the window or dangle some rusty chains.

BLACK: Roosevelt is a far classier ghost. He would use a microphone, sit by the hearth, and flick his cigarette holder.

WARREN: Equal patrons?

BLACK: Does it matter in the end?

WARREN: Order an omelet. I can't stand eating alone.

BLACK: Fine. You have to break eggs to make an omelet. Flag the waiter, Earl.

WARREN: You've been on the court sixteen years.

BLACK: I lost count after Vinson died. Maybe I'm still in shock about his passing.

WARREN: You want to pay homage to Vinson.

BLACK: "Homage?" I wouldn't express things exactly like that.

WARREN: You and I agree.

BLACK: We do. The Deep South might close every single public school to block integration, but that has no bearing on my decision. "With all deliberate speed" can mean a thousand different things to each town and city. To a wife in bed, it has its own connotation.

WARREN: Look who just walked in.

BLACK: J Edgar Hoover?

WARREN: Turn to your left.

BLACK: Strom Thurmond?

WARREN: Certainly looks like the "young" Senator.

BLACK: Who is he with?

WARREN: Some woman. Not his wife.

BLACK: Good looking gal?

WARREN: His wife is attractive.

BLACK: Not his wife, the lady here...

WARREN: Very attractive redhead, but don't look now. He's staring at us.

BLACK: You want to know my legal definition of a Dixiecrat? *(Pause)* A charming plantation democrat who has a confederate flag firmly up his rectum.

WARREN: You were once in the Klan, Hugo.

BLACK: Youthful indiscretion, naturally.

WARREN: Enough good judgment to earn your way into Hell.

BLACK: Probably. But my intention is clear. Just as I thought we had to reverse the lower-court Brown decision, we need to deny the Virginia brief asking for "an indeterminable period." Virginia's stance is thoroughly gloomy and uncooperative. School integration has to have a pressing timetable, or the whole enterprise is a farce.

WARREN: I agree. Felix agrees. With a little more luck, perhaps all nine of us will agree again.

BLACK: I worry that Stanley Reed still abides by segregation.

WARREN: Worry is a useless emotion.

BLACK: Only if you portray God Almighty.

WARREN: Stanley is unpredictable, and a pain in the ass, so don't count him out.

BLACK: Do you have a crystal ball, Earl?

WARREN: Well, I should. We overruled *Plessy* beautifully.

BLACK: But Jim Crow behavior won't disappear for years to come.

WARREN: Here comes Strom.

BLACK: Toward us?

WARREN: Yes.

BLACK: What a horrible day.

WARREN: It started without a hitch.

BLACK: To hell with the omelet, let's call a cab.

SENATOR: Good afternoon, distinguished jurists of our high court.

WARREN/BLACK: Good afternoon, Senator.

SENATOR: I felt compelled to saunter over, but you must please forgive my rudeness.

WARREN: No rudeness taken.

SENATOR: I hear the cheese omelets are excellent.

BLACK: Really?

SENATOR: Thurgood Marshall's recommendation to me, actually.

WARREN: Are you alone?

SENATOR: I'm never alone, Mister Chief Justice. That's my office manager in a magnificent chiffon dress. And her salary is far from royal. How do you suppose she underwrites herself?

BLACK: She moonlights as a ballroom dance instructor? Ten cents a dance...ten cents a dance...

WARREN: How's your wife?

SENATOR: Very well, thank you. Jean's back in South Carolina. How's yours?

WARREN: Quite fine, thank you.

SENATOR: *(To* BLACK*)* We are elite members of the ex-governors society. Representing the best of California and South Carolina.

BLACK: Jobs change, but the dance remains the same.

WARREN: The Senator is very fit. An avid swimmer, I believe.

SENATOR: And no alcoholic beverages, Mister Chief Justice. The same waist size since college days. *(Pause)* Well, please do excuse me. I know you scholars have very important business to discuss. *(He exits.)*

BLACK: He and I are both southerners, Earl.

WARREN: What's your point?

BLACK: Our history and legacy seals our respective fates. Below the Mason-Dixon line, there's a deep seated fear of miscegenation.

WARREN: That's an ugly word to my ears.

BLACK: There's no other word more apt.

WARREN: I think that fear is in every city and state.

BLACK: Yes, yet in the South there are so many generations of blacks and whites sharing biological ancestry. Two races racing along parallel lines.

WARREN: Two races falling off parallel lines.

BLACK: Exactly. And this clown Strom Thurmond has to appeal to his constituency, no matter how tolerant he feels inside. That is the human paradox. Prescribe utopian dreams, and see the hateful racial wall before us grow taller.

WARREN: I don't think we are begging this nation to lose all reality.

BLACK: Now Earl, ask yourself who's kidding whom?

WARREN: I ask myself that every day.

BLACK: You're equating sweeping social justice with some idealization not on this soil.

WARREN: We make the effort to move forward, Hugo. Why? Because we who sit up high on the Supreme Court are safely beyond the will and the whim of the voting public.

BLACK: Is this your revelation for today?

WARREN: I feel this almost every day.

BLACK: As do I. Tell me then, Earl, now that we're on our third drink—do you feel superior to "the voting public"?

WARREN: No.

BLACK: I do.

WARREN: Then perhaps you're more honest than me.

(End of Scene)

Scene Three

(LEZA's second direct address)

LEZA: After the initial Brown decision, the Supreme Court had pursued a greater course of integration in public parks, interstate rest stops, court houses, libraries and other public buildings, and practically all commercial public facilities. To disclose the racial make-up of a candidate in an election ballot became illegal. Sexual contact between the races was no longer unlawful. Laws which forbade marriages between

blacks and whites were struck down. *(Pause)* My
parents came from the west—Oakland, California
to be specific—and were spared that prohibition.
But I still sense the pain of what they had to experience
each and every day of their lives *(Pause)* Curiously
enough, the Court's directives desegregated much of
the south—parks, restaurants, buses, sports arenas—
yet public schools—our precious humble public schools
still were under the spell of Jim Crow codes. *(Pause)*
I ran into Essie Mae a few years ago in Los Angeles. She
didn't recognize my face, I put on a lot of weight over
the decades, despite a thousand expensive diets. She
was courteous to me and I reminded her of my favorite
memories from her classroom. Essie Mae laughed and
then hid her mouth with her solid hand. I don't believe
in coincidences. She was happy to know that I became a
teacher *(Pause)* I made a big point in my classroom the
other day. However it escaped my students. In July
of 1955, Judge John Parker of the Federal Circuit
reviewing the South Carolina school case, opined,
"The Constitution, in other words, does not require
integration. It merely forbids discrimination." *(Pause)*
According to Parker, the Constitution does not forbid
such discrimination as occurs as a result of voluntary
action. It merely forbids the use of government power
to enforce segregation. *(Pause)* This legal reasoning,
known as the "Parker Doctrine" was subscribed too
eagerly by the federal "Dixie" courts *(Pause)* I can't
hazard a guess how utterly conflicted Thurgood
Marshall was at this juncture.

(End of scene)

Scene Four

(Washington DC. April 1955)

(THURGOOD MARSHALL's *office, a call between* MARSHALL *and* CARL MURPHY, *Publisher of* Afro-American*)*

MURPHY: *(On the phone)* Carl Murphy.

MARSHALL: *(On the phone)* Hello, Carl. Hey, how ya doin'?

MURPHY: Fine, thank you.

MARSHALL: What do you think of Tuesday's decision?

MURPHY: Better than a case of hemorrhoids. Well, I was disappointed in the beginning when I read the first paragraph, and then I read all the good faith, deliberate speed, prompt start bullshit.

MARSHALL: I'm wrestling with it too.

MURPHY: I'm not surprised, Thurgood.

MARSHALL: Well?

MURPHY: We live in a very white land.

MARSHALL: Shit, tell me about it.

MURPHY: It's so white, I can't tell when it's snowing. And I'm dreaming of crazy colored rainbows. *(Pause)* I'm a son of Baltimore, for better or worse.

MARSHALL: So is that literary crank H.L. Mencken.

MURPHY: More a racist than a crank. Son-of-a-bitch...

MARSHALL: Mencken was under the spell of Nietzsche. What can you expect?

MURPHY: I'm also a child of Harvard.

MARSHALL: It helps to come from a family with money.

MURPHY: But when I applied to John Hopkins University for post-graduate work, I was rejected due to my color. I'll never forgive Johns Hopkin and I have such love/hate for my town. That's why I sued the Baltimore & Ohio Railroad for forcing me to sit away from white folks on a ferry. I sued the damn city when a cop arrested me wrongly for a traffic accident. My daddy made our Baltimore family the most prominent of this race and his weekly newspaper changed the face of black America.

MARSHALL: Without you, Carl, the N A A C P chapter would be abysmal here.

MURPHY: We have to fight our people's own timidity.

MARSHALL: There are no timetables.

MURPHY: I realize. The only practical timetables are in publishing.

MARSHALL: How do we deal with this shit?

MURPHY: A little mojo wouldn't hurt. The older I get, the more pragmatic I become. Don't beat yourself up, my friend.

MARSHALL: "Good faith, deliberate speed, prompt start..."

MURPHY: We begin with a little step. I'll tell my readers the very same thing. (Pause) I come to the conclusion that we got ourselves a package.

MARSHALL: That's what we've been saying.

MURPHY: That's absolutely what I think. They didn't put a time limit on it, but my thought is that we can go with this.

MARSHALL: I'm sure of it. I was telling the guys up here—the guys kept on woofin' and I told them—I said, you know, some people want most of the hog, other people insist on having the whole hog, and then there are some people who want the hog, the hair, and the rice on the hair. What the hell! The more I think about, I think it's a damned good decision!

MURPHY: I talked to Carter before. He said *Plessy V Ferguson* is out and Earl Warren has cut the ground from under them by saying if you have segregation in these schools, it's unlawful. Therefore, the burden is on you to get 'em lawful.

MARSHALL: And the damn laws have to yield! They've got to yield to the Constitution. And yield means yield! Yield means give up!

MURPHY: I'm not enthusiastically happy, Thurgood, but I'm happy.

MARSHALL: Are you happy?

MURPHY: I'm happy.

MARSHALL: Are you happy?

MURPHY: I'm happy.

MARSHALL: Well, you know, the more you think of it, it had to be anti-climactic... hell, I've spent so many years on this.

MURPHY: What are you going to do, Thurgood?

MARSHALL: We'll file state by state. Each municipality which refuses to integrate, we'll yank their ass into court. We'll march tall through the courts from Maryland through Georgia, just as Sherman's army had marched through the Confederacy.

MURPHY: I don't see any reason why, if we beat Virginia and Carolina, the rest of them aren't going to wake up.

MARSHALL: You damn right they are! You can say all you want, but those white crackers are going to get tired of having Negro lawyers beating 'em every day in court. They're going to get mighty tired of it.

* * *

LEZA: Essie Mae had the privilege of being reared in the North where life was more progressive, more tolerant perhaps, and she had private financial support from one of the most elite sons of Southern white families. I told this to my class. Essie Mae had lighter skin than many black children. Some say she even bears a remarkable resemblance to her famous white father. The school recess bell rang. My kids just flew out of the room. All but one, that is. Manuel Diego sat still in the back row. Manuel has jet black eyes and he walks very slowly. And he told me to go on. He was listening. *(Pause)* The black children Essie Mae once knew back in South Carolina went to extremely poor school houses that lacked toilets and books and teachers. Some of the black children Essie Mae knew never made it past the sixth grade. Essie Mae had her share of good luck growing up yet I can imagine the profound pain in her young heart. In a manner of speaking, she was the talented, unacknowledged daughter of all Southern white gentlemen. And Manuel quietly rose from his seat.

(End of scene)

Scene Five

*(*SENATOR *and* ESSIE MAE *in Senate office)*

SENATOR: When I saw you for the first time, Essie-Mae, you were so stunned. We both were, my dear girl. I'll never forget driving to your campus and I'll never forget how frightened I was to make contact. I don't readily admit my fears, particularly in public. It would mean the death of my career as certain as God is my

witness. I had my driver circle your college campus
for hours before I found the nerve to get out of the car.
Yet I felt so much better at the end of the day. I asked
God for *His* help. I asked my wife for *her* help. I asked
you for *your* help. Our meeting nearly ending at that
moment. You saw me shed some tears, didn't you?

ESSIE MAE: Yes.

SENATOR: And I can count on one hand the times I ever
cried as a grown man.

ESSIE MAE: All living things do cry, sir.

SENATOR: Your mother and I didn't have much in
common, but we were drawn together in a profoundly
powerful way. See, my Daddy was very stern with me,
but he loved me in his own way. And I had to respect
that. Still, I did many wild things behind his back,
because he would often give me a lickin' with a hickory
branch. My Daddy knew I took a fancy to your mother.
I really think he knew. But my mind and my heart were
a million miles away from that hickory stick. Your
mother was an extremely beautiful woman, Essie Mae.
Photographs just don't do justice. And she had such
warmth in her open hands. She had healing hands.
Anything she touched was given more life. Like
sunbeams after a spring shower. I should have had
more self-discipline. I wish I had better words to
describe what I felt for her. I have a torrent of words
when I speak in public, Essie-Mae. But in private, with
you, knowing what we both know...my tongue just gets
so dry and defeated. The Thurman family defines so
much of what makes South Carolina a proud, historic
state. In my heart and in my mind, you too are a
member of the Thurmans.

ESSIE MAE: No, I'm not.

SENATOR: In God's view, you definitely are.

ESSIE MAE: Maybe in God's view.

SENATOR: You do believe in Him?

ESSIE MAE: Yes.

SENATOR: Good.

ESSIE MAE: Why did He create colored people?

SENATOR: God sees life in so many glorious varieties.

ESSIE MAE: That's not what I asked, sir.

SENATOR: You know, colored folk are closer to God.

ESSIE MAE: How?

SENATOR: Because colored folk work the fields and God is more present in the farms. Colored folk sing hymns and Gospel much finer than whites. Colored folk rock in God's deepest rhythms. And colored folk sense paradise much more than other folk. In poverty, God fills the heart. All proving that you are closer to God. And I envy you for the purity of your heart, Essie Mae.

(She removes a wrapped present.)

SENATOR: What is that?

ESSIE MAE: A gift for you.

SENATOR: Whatever for?

ESSIE MAE: It's your birthday.

SENATOR: No, no, darling. I was born in December. December fifth.

ESSIE MAE: Oh my gosh.

SENATOR: My dear, I never make a big deal out of my birthday. So what difference does it make? I'll accept any present of yours, any day of the year. But you know what will simply thrill me right now?

ESSIE MAE: What?

SENATOR: Your singing voice. Your mellifluous voice.

ESSIE MAE: I only sing in the church choir.

SENATOR: You never sing for your aunts?

ESSIE MAE: Sometimes.

SENATOR: Essie Mae, won't you please sing for me today?

ESSIE MAE: Here? Now?

SENATOR: Please. I would be so honored.

ESSIE MAE: What should I sing?

SENATOR: Anything your heart would like.

ESSIE MAE: I feel so awkward, Senator.

SENATOR: Stop calling me, Senator.

ESSIE MAE: I'm so sorry.

SENATOR: Do you sing in the shower?

ESSIE MAE: No.

SENATOR: What do you like singing for your choir?

ESSIE MAE: Hymns mostly. Sometimes *Amazing Grace.*

SENATOR: Wonderful. Sing that, my dear.

(She does. She sings several bars, first very tentatively and building with feeling.)

ESSIE MAE: Amazing Grace, how sweet the sound
That saved a wretch like me
I once was lost, but now I'm found
Twas Grace that set me free

SENATOR: That was heavenly, Essie Mae. I felt tears building up like a rising tide.

(End of scene)

Scene Six

(MARSHALL *reading a report to a Northern chapter of the N A A C P)*

MARSHALL: Of course, I wish that President Eisenhower would assume a truly heroic position on school integration. I would even settle if he would take a defined position, to say the least. And I know that inside he is a decent man. He could help instruct the nation in a million ways. But this president, this W W Two hero, chooses to hide like a deer in the woods. *(Pause)* I want very much to conclude this talk early because I realize you want to beat the rush hour traffic. Again, I want to thank this Northern Chapter of the N A A C P for sponsoring this benefit and I want to thank you for contributing so generously to the N A A C P. Believe me, every dollar helps enormously. So I have one more thing to read aloud from a school investigator, Matthew Whitehead: *(Pause)* "In Clarendon County, South Carolina, open galvanized buckets with tarnished dippers inserted furnished drinking water for the children who attended the two Negro elementary schools whereas the children in the two white schools were rid of this heath hazard by having fountains. Each Negro school had a roof which leaked when it had rained.

   For the two white schools...there is bus transportation available. Although the three Negro schools are located in isolated, unimproved areas, the children have no transportation whatsoever. At the Rambay school, the investigator Matthew Whitehead found two little Negro boys in the first grade, age six, walked each day a round trip of ten miles to get to school.

   The white schools have a clean lunch room with a paid attendant and other workers in charge, but

nowhere in the Negro schools could one find any signs
of a lunch room.

Janitorial services were found in both white schools,
but no such services in the Negro schools.

At the Rambay School, there was not a single desk
in the whole school. In contrast, the white schools had
a desk for every child. And every desk has a flower.

At the Summerton Elementary School for whites there
was a spacious auditorium for aesthetics, assemblies,
films, etc.... At the Summerton High School, there was
a combination gymnasium which had excellent
provisions for all activities.

At the three nearby Negro schools... *(Long pause)* I'll
just end here. You all get the drift. Thank you so kindly.

(End of scene)

Scene Seven

*(Washington DC restaurant. WARREN is seated alone and
the SENATOR approaches.)*

SENATOR: Excuse me, Mister Chief Justice. May I
please join you for a brief moment? It seemed like only
yesterday when we were all running on that national
ticket in '48. We do have something in common—
our mild but sustained aversion to Harry Truman.

WARREN: I've never disliked Mister Truman.

SENATOR: Well, yes, I've learned to like the former
President now that he's back in *Kansas.*

WARREN: *Missouri.*

SENATOR: *(Slight chuckle)* I have been a great admirer
of the High Court and I have been a steady observer of
the profound decisions of late. I am only a man from
the South and life in our nation's capital is still quite
daunting. You and your colleagues have changed the

face of our society, as I'm certain you know the problems we are experiencing between the races and between societies. I worry at times about the infusion of communist ideas and communist instigators and Jewish activists and general discord to my cultured South.

WARREN: Come to the point, Senator.

SENATOR: The point? The point being—how the hell will the High Court—with all due respect—enforce these new decisions when even Eisenhower is uncommitted?

(End of Scene)

Scene Eight

(September 1957. MARSHALL, visiting Little Rock, Arkansas, is on the phone with MURPHY.)

MARSHALL: Hey, Carl, I'm calling from Arkansas.

MURPHY: I figured you'd be there sooner or later.

MARSHALL: I thought you would be here.

MURPHY: I can't leave Baltimore just yet. I'm swamped with work.

MARSHALL: It's not looking pretty down in Little Rock.

MURPHY: You could call F T D and ship over a truckload of the sweetest flowers, ain't going to make any difference. It stinks to high heaven. Plus, you got the biggest jerk in the governor's office, Thurgood.

MARSHALL: *(Laughing)* Orval Faubus is a buffoon, I'll grant you that.

MURPHY: Faubus warned that "blood will run in the streets".

MARSHALL: And I think he wants to make his prophesy self-fulfilling. *(Pause)* You got Daisy Bates waking up one morning to a cross flaming in her front yard. You know, she's the N A A C P chapter president. She's got a family, for Christsake! She was threatened before. We're not just talking about the Klan, mind you. Young white kids are throwing rocks into her window too. All because she brought in nine black students to Central High. Today's note told her that the rocks will become dynamite by the end of the week. *(Pause)* Carl, I had thought... hell, we'd all thought, that once we got the Brown case, the thing was going to be over. This is three years later!

MURPHY: We weren't nave, but I fell into that fool's trap too, Thurgood.

MARSHALL: So Central High opens and the National Guard surround the school. The Guard's full of the good ol' boys and they aren't trained for civil disturbances. Hell, they're not even potty trained. This is gasoline on an open fire. And one teen, Elizabeth Eckford, went by herself instead of joining Daisy's group. Not that safety in numbers would have changed the picture. The damn soldiers dropped their bayonets at her and the poor girl was almost killed by the rabid, white mob.

MURPHY: What are you going do?

MARSHALL: I got to get Eisenhower into this dog fight.

MURPHY: And off the golf course?

MARSHALL: I was lucky with local court. We convinced Judge Davies to rule in favor of the school plan despite the scare tactics from the governor's office. I know Faubus sent a telegram to the White House asking the President not to intervene despite the court order. So I had the N A A C P telegram Eisenhower and issue a flurry of press releases. But that's not enough.

MURPHY: I know.

MARSHALL: We must be body and spirit in the public eye because Eisenhower is afraid of this whole miserable thing. *(Pause)* I'm going to Daisy Bates's house under escort.

MURPHY: Take care, Thurgood.

MARSHALL: It's a risk, I know.

MURPHY: What do you think Eisenhower will do?

MARSHALL: Probably he'll have the Justice Department go to court seeking an injunction to pull the Guard away from the school.

MURPHY: That only slaps Faubus' wrist.

MARSHALL: I know. Faubus is prepared to ask for a one year delay to integrate Central. To calm the white community as if they need balm for the soul. In my heart I know the kids in Central, the white kids, will be decent with the eight black teens. I fear that Faubus is fanning the flames and not even the 101st Airborne will bring peace in Little Rock.

MURPHY: You think conditions would change once Eisenhower leaves office?

MARSHALL: I don't know and I don't intend to wait another four goddamn years.

MURPHY: Thurgood, this is the angriest I've ever heard you.

MARSHALL: No it isn't. *(Pause)* Carl, I was drinking with a lawyer friend Branton in a local pool hall. A young black guy, smoking a cigar and carrying a pool cue, came over to me and said, "Hey, lawyer-man, you know anything about this shit, where you come back after you die?" *(Pause)* I asked him if he was talking about *reincarnation*. The man nodded and said, "Yeah." I told him that I knew more about the law than about

spiritual affairs. Then he shoots back at me, "Well, if
you find anybody that has anything to do with it, tell
'em when I come back to earth, I don't give a good
damn what it is, whether I become a new man or
a woman, a horse, a cow, a squirrel whatever it is,
let it be *fucking white!*"

MURPHY: And there it is, Thurgood.

MARSHALL: So put in print in your authoritative
Afro-American journal— "We are going to drop all
other cases nationwide and the full legal staff of the
N A A C P will concentrate every bit of energy on
Little Rock until Hell freezes over. The kids will be
back safely in school in September." *(Beat)* Or I will
go *ballistic.*

LEZA: And believe me, white folk did not want
Marshall to go ballistic. Three years later in January,
1960, Senator Thurmond suffers the first great shock
of his life.

(End of scene)

Scene Nine

(January 1960. The SENATOR's *Senate office. The* SENATOR
is on the phone.)

SENATOR: *(To an unidentified politician)* Listen, Charlie.
Please shut that trap. My mind is simply not on
business and I don't know what to tell you. I have no
heart for anything. Grieving is a hellish predicament
since you know me as a man of great action. *(Pause)*
Just tell your dear, patient folks that their concerns are
clearly top drawer and, with Godspeed, your trust in
me will be well placed. *(Pause)* ou don't need to pay
a visit. I truly mean that, Charlie. I quite understand.
Thank you. Yes. Bye now.

(Looking up, he spots ESSIE MAE.*)*

SENATOR: My gosh, I didn't know you were standing there. How long?

ESSIE MAE: Just a minute or two.

SENATOR: I thought you couldn't come.

ESSIE MAE: Things had changed.

SENATOR: Is your husband with you?

ESSIE MAE: No.

SENATOR: I know I look haggard and just plain awful.

ESSIE MAE: Not really, sir.

SENATOR: Please have a seat.

ESSIE MAE: Thank you. *(Selecting a chair)*

SENATOR: She was buried at Bethany Cemetery, on a lovely hill under tall elm trees.

ESSIE MAE: Yes, I know. I've read a full account in the paper.

SENATOR: Elms are so stately and peaceful. Lyndon Johnson led a delegation of southern senators. He and I patched up our differences quite suddenly. *(Pause)* You would have liked Jean.

ESSIE MAE: I met your wife once.

SENATOR: That's right.

ESSIE MAE: Did she know about me?

SENATOR: Of course. I told her about you soon after our wedding.

ESSIE MAE: I'm at a loss for words.

SENATOR: We met in 1941 when Jean's father took her and her high school class to watch a court session in Barnwell County. I was the presiding judge, Essie Mae,

and I immediately took notice of her "special light".
I saw her again five years later at her Winthrop college.
Jean was her senior class president and I was the
governor-elect. I was forty-four and felt it was the
proper time to start a family. My office sent word to
her to consider working for my team. *(Pause)* Well,
she reported to work July first, two weeks shy of her
twenty-first birthday. *(Pause)* She was part of my
entourage that went to the National Governors
Conference in Salt Lake. Jean stayed in the hotel
room typing out a boring speech while I hosted
Governor Earl Warren's daughters to a rodeo.
The following day Jean teased the hell out of me about
dating the Warren girls! It was at that point that I knew
she loved me. *(Pause)* Two months later Jean wrote her
folks about our plans to make things permanent. So I
proposed to Jean formally by dictating a letter to her:
*My darling Jean, You have proved to be a most efficient and
capable secretary, and the high caliber of your work has
impressed me very much. I regret to inform you that your
services will be discontinued as of the last day of this month.*
Then in the next paragraph, I confessed how much I
loved her and asked for her hand. She closed her steno
pad and left the room. I was absolutely crushed that
she was going to reject me. I just cannot stand rejection.
Well, Jean kept me in dire suspense until the end
of the day. She had typed out my letter with her
corrections added, and typed out her acceptance.
My dearest Strom, yes! My love always, Jean
(He leaves desk and crosses.) Jean's health changed
overnight. Last summer she began to tire easily and
her concentration was failing. As a result, Jean ran
into a truck and got by without a scratch.
It was then that I thought she had a guardian angel
for life. However, in August she collapsed in our
apartment. More seizures had followed. It was a

goddamn brain tumor. After surgery, she soon became partly paralyzed. *(Pause)* I'm sorry to just go on like this.

ESSIE MAE: Please. I understand.

SENATOR: Mind you, she was only thirty three.

ESSIE MAE: I knew she was very young.

SENATOR: I could not believe a woman this beautiful, bright, and vital could be stolen right out of our lives. I couldn't understand why God would allow such a tragedy. I was crying like a baby so wild about my lost Jean

ESSIE MAE: The nation will sorely miss her.

SENATOR: My deepest regret—you know—we couldn't have children.

ESSIE MAE: I'm sorry.

SENATOR: I have always loved your sincerity, Essie Mae.

ESSIE MAE: Having children is a blessing.

SENATOR: Indeed.

ESSIE MAE: At least for me. And I thank God every week in church.

SENATOR: I can see that plainly on your face.

ESSIE MAE: They need to see you.

SENATOR: Yes. *(Pause)* Your children?

ESSIE MAE: And when they get older, I have to put matters in the right perspective.

SENATOR: Am I making that hard for you?

ESSIE MAE: I don't know.

SENATOR: Some days I have a firm hold on my beliefs. Other days are quite nettlesome. *(Pause)* I don't think I'm being very clear. What I mean to say is that in

Washington we are very exposed and very public.
Far more now than when I was the state governor.

ESSIE MAE: These are your grandchildren, sir.

SENATOR: Yes, you're absolutely right.

ESSIE MAE: I'm not asking too much.

SENATOR: No, you're not.

ESSIE MAE: I can't read your mind.

SENATOR: You must sense that I'm on the verge of tears.

(She nods.)

SENATOR: Are you in town for the weekend?

ESSIE MAE: Yes.

SENATOR: Good.

ESSIE MAE: Can I help you?

SENATOR: I certainly hope so. *(Pause. Long sigh)* Let me
ring you at your hotel.

ESSIE MAE: Actually, I'm staying with friends. My
children came with me.

SENATOR: Then do call me at my home number tonight,
Essie Mae. We can proceed as best we can. We are a
discreet family, after all, and I am determined to meet
your darling children this weekend.

(End of scene)

LEZA: Five years later—1965—in July, Marshall,
now a federal court judge, is in his chambers and
receives a surprising phone call.

Scene Ten

(July 1965. MARSHALL *in his court chambers receives a call from* PRESIDENT LYNDON JOHNSON. *We don't see* JOHNSON, *or we just see a silhouette of L B J.)*

MARSHALL: Thurgood Marshall speaking, sir.

JOHNSON: Hello, Judge Marshall. Do you have a few minutes?

MARSHALL: Yes, Mister President, but of course.

JOHNSON: How is your day?

MARSHALL: Hectic.

JOHNSON: How is your wife?

MARSHALL: Just fine, sir.

JOHNSON: Good. Are you enjoying sitting on the appeals court?

MARSHALL: I like the work, Mister President.

JOHNSON: Be honest, Thurgood.

JOHNSON: The cases can be dreary...

JOHNSON: *(Teasing)* Dreary or weary, you say?

MARSHALL: ...but I think my contributions are lasting and monumental.

JOHNSON: It was so nice to see you the other day at the White House ceremony.

MARSHALL: Indeed.

JOHNSON: For a relatively young man, you are fast becoming part of American history.

MARSHALL: I'm not all that young, sir.

JOHNSON: I never had a moment to thank you years ago for rallying the N A A C P to support wholeheartedly my senate race. And I'm the kind of guy that pays attention to these wonderful deeds. I keep a notebook inside my head and the pages get thumbed every damn night. Which is to say that I have admired you from afar and that I hold the N A A C P to the highest light. When did we first meet?

MARSHALL: I would say going all the way back to the 1940s in Texas.

JOHNSON: You were fighting the all-white primary system.

MARSHALL: That's right, sir.

JOHNSON: Well, you are a smart, tenacious fighter and it seems you win more battles than not.

MARSHALL: There are battles, Mr. President, and there are wars.

JOHNSON: Very true. And we both know the distinction. You handled the Supreme Court appearances quite well. You took the proper and dignified measures to each southern state in due course and on *your timetable.* I respect your pragmatism and your sense of an integrated American society. I know that the term, "gradualism" can mean many things to many people.

MARSHALL: From my end, I made the word a forward step. It was not a word of stigma to me *on my timetable.*

JOHNSON: Let's cut to the chase then. You are my kind of man, Thurgood. You truly are. You are hero in my book. And I put my full faith into your character. So listen carefully—I want you to be my solicitor general. I know it pays a little less than on the court of appeals, and I know you like black robes, and I know you have a lovely lifetime appointment with a guaranteed pension. *(Pause)* But like I say, *I want you, no, I need you to be my solicitor general.*

MARSHALL: *(Genuinely shocked by the offer)* I...I don't know what to say.

JOHNSON: You have mighty fine legal skills and none of your hunred or so rulings on the second circuit have ever been overturned. I find that impressive, Thurgood. You would be the first black to serve that position. And you'd be the top black official ever to serve the U S government. *(Pause)* Don't worry about the confirmation hearings 'cause I know how to handle these fools in congress on this one. We'll have a bumpy ride, but nothing to lose sleep over. *(Pause)* Now I know you have a *particular hankering* to serve on the high court and that would be in no uncertain terms, *a supreme wish.* I also know that the press will make all sorts of conjectures about this being your springboard to the Supreme Court. But the solicitor general is all I have up my sleeve today. So my friend, even if it looks like one, this isn't a *quid pro quo.* I'm a Texan. I'm not assuming any obligations and you shouldn't assume any expectations for a grander office. And say goodbye to New York. I expect you to move your wife Cissy and the boys to Washington. No commuting whatsoever! I suppose I'm as clear as mud to you. *(Pause)* I think that's all I have to say today to you, Judge Marshall.

MARSHALL: Well, Mister President. I'll have to think it over.

JOHNSON: Of course, take all the time you need to think it over with the missus. *(Pause)* I'll call you tomorrow for an answer.

(End of scene)

LEZA: *(Ironic)* Yes, L B J had a lot of *charm and deference.* *(Pause)* In Thurmond's office during one of the warmest days in Washington.

(It's historically one year earlier.*)*

Scene Eleven

(The SENATOR's *office. July 1964.* ESSIE MAE *and the* SENATOR *are in the middle of a conversation. The* SENATOR *is without his suit jacket.)*

SENATOR: It certainly is hot outside. But I think I just interrupted you?

ESSIE MAE: I'm not a young girl any more.

SENATOR: In my eyes, you will always be young.

ESSIE MAE: Actually, I want to show my age, warts and all.

SENATOR: Really?

ESSIE MAE: I like the wrinkles under my hairline.

SENATOR: Then you are unlike most women I know.

ESSIE MAE: I am not like other women, sir.

SENATOR: I know.

ESSIE MAE: The country is changing.

SENATOR: In what way?

ESSIE MAE: There are greater freedoms for young people and for disadvantaged people.

SENATOR: All to the good.

ESSIE MAE: I think it began with President Kennedy's assassination. We're all a little stunned and it's not quite a year.

SENATOR: Yes. Every man, woman and child has been traumatized.

ESSIE MAE: And perhaps the country will address many more social issues now.

SENATOR: I have to say, Kennedy was ill prepared to move a great deal of domestic bills through Congress. I personally think it was his elite New England upbringing and the wealthy family estate. You know his daddy was a bootlegger during Prohibition. Whereas Johnson did not come from privilege and has more savvy than a carnival barker and the will power of a marauding rhinoceros.

ESSIE MAE: I had hoped that you would lend some support toward the Civil Rights Act.

SENATOR: Why?

ESSIE MAE: Isn't it obvious?

SENATOR: I'm surprised you would even mention the subject. We do best outside of such talk.

ESSIE MAE: Maybe I'm saying this on behalf of my mother.

SENATOR: I see.

ESSIE MAE: Do you?

SENATOR: The Civil Rights Act is a severely flawed bill and the very idea of the bill serves the Communists and their propaganda efforts. The bill is redundant. States have their own democratic mechanisms to correct the tensions between the races.

ESSIE MAE: You know that's untrue.

SENATOR: No, I don't.

ESSIE MAE: Well, you still are in a position to change how the country will go.

SENATOR: I wish that were true. But twenty-one conservative Southern Democrats in the Senate are a significant consensus. And on the other team, you have Goldwater leading a good many conservative Republicans also in opposition to the Civil Rights Act. The essential problem with the bill was how sweeping and reckless it would be. Look, I'm nearly ready to quit the Democratic Party forever. I felt this in 1948 and now even stronger. There really has to be a realignment of

social thought and practicality—but L B J is simply
guilt-tripping this tired country. *(Pause)* Please let's
not focus on politics.

ESSIE MAE: I just hope that one day...

SENATOR: I know, I know. And that day will come soon
enough. *(Silence)* Essie Mae, I'm truly saddened by the
passing of Julius.

ESSIE MAE: Thank you.

SENATOR: What a lovely husband he was to you and a
magnificent father to your children.

ESSIE MAE: You know that we had married in secret.

SENATOR: No.

ESSIE MAE: His family only knew about it afterwards.
That was Julius's way of doing things—quietly and
modestly.

SENATOR: Julius fought hard for several good causes.
(Pause) He was ill for quite some time.

ESSIE MAE: Yes.

SENATOR: Did he suffer?

ESSIE MAE: He did.

SENATOR: God look over his soul. *(Pause)* How are your
children?

ESSIE MAE: They're coping as best they can.

SENATOR: Please convey my love and condolences
to your children. *(Pause)* He was an extremely bright
individual, Essie Mae. I knew that when Julius returned
to Savannah to practice law, his career would flourish.

ESSIE MAE: In part due to your efforts.

SENATOR: Nonsense. He was quite giving to civic
groups, including the local N A A C P which he

headed. His achievements were many and I know that he reached the pinnacle with the teacher pay case with Kravitch. *(Pause)* Now we both have suffered the loss of a spouse and it's terribly hard to move on.

ESSIE MAE: Yes, it is.

SENATOR: I'm glad you had the time to journey here.

ESSIE MAE: Actually, I had to come. I didn't think a letter was appropriate. *(Pause)* Our family problems are considerable. Julius's death benefits are not sufficient by any standard, and we're experiencing a terrible drain on our savings—despite my teaching income.

SENATOR: I see.

ESSIE MAE: I'm embarrassed to be saying this.

SENATOR: Don't be.

ESSIE MAE: Frankly, it's been many years since I had asked for assistance.

SENATOR: I don't remember.

ESSIE MAE: Believe me.

SENATOR: I do, dear. And you must not panic.

ESSIE MAE: I'm trying to be calm.

SENATOR: Are you asking for some annuity over a span of years? Or will a single payment suffice?

ESSIE MAE: I think an annuity would be wiser.

SENATOR: All right.

ESSIE MAE: At least until all the children have grown.

(SENATOR puts on his suit jacket which was straddled over his chair. The jacket looks to be a tight fit.)

SENATOR: And their college years too. *(Pause)* Then at some point, the checks will have to come from a third party outside of this city, Essie Mae, and that will be easier for all of us.

ESSIE MAE: Fine. *(Pause)* You're putting on weight, sir.

SENATOR: I still swim four times a week, but I think the pool is getting smaller.

ESSIE MAE: Maybe you're enjoying your share of desserts?

SENATOR: At my age—sixty-one—I'm allowed one dessert every evening. It's in my personal Magna Carta.

ESSIE MAE: I eat dessert too.

SENATOR: How is your teaching?

ESSIE MAE: Going well. I like teenagers.

SENATOR: But that God-awful music.

ESSIE MAE: You don't enjoy the Ronettes or the Beatles?

SENATOR: Honestly, I don't know the Beatles from the boll weevils.

ESSIE MAE: *(Laughing)* The Beatles are from England. The Ronettes are from Detroit - Motown. *(Pause)* I have to ask you something else, sir.

SENATOR: *(A twinge of impatience)* What?

ESSIE MAE: Did you really wrestle down Senator Yarborough of Texas the other day?

SENATOR: Yes.

ESSIE MAE: Why, if I may ask?

SENATOR: Because he's a goddamn asshole. *(Pause)* I was trying to prevent a quorum from confirming a maleficent director's appointment. He thought he was being cute and made a little scene in the hallway. It's not just that Yarborough's a flaming activist, but he's always goading me to do the wrong thing. He grabbed

my hand and tugged me toward the committee room.
I told him I knew judo from the army. I got him on the
floor first. We were in a blasted mule race all over again.

(Escorting ESSIE MAE *to the door)*

SENATOR: And I truly whooped his liberal ass.

(End of scene)

Scene Twelve

*(*LEZA *opens a Congressional archival book.)*

LEZA: In just a few years Lyndon Johnson was prepared
to nominate Thurgood Marshall to the Supreme Court.
July 1967. The last three court appointments, Byron
White, Arthur Goldberg, and Abe Fortas had gone *from
nomination to confirmation under two weeks.* But this time,
the F B I was asked by the senate to check on Marshall's
alleged ties to Communists. Many of the southern
senators on the Judiciary Committee were prepared to
kill the nomination. A representative of Louisiana
branded Marshall as a "scamp" and a "cheat" in the
Congressional Record. However, the F B I's J Edgar
Hoover gave Marshall a clean bill of health. The delays
with the hearing gave the segregationist press ample
time to take shots at Marshall. Other media in and
around the nation handed Marshall strong words of
support. Senator James Eastland from Mississippi was
the Committee Chairman.

Scene Thirteen

(July 1967, Washington. Senate confirmation hearing for
MARSHALL's *Supreme Court nomination. Unseen to the
audience, the* CHAIRMAN, SENATOR JAMES EASTLAND *of*

Mississippi calls on the SENATOR *to begin his questions for* MARSHALL.*)*

CHAIRMAN: *(Off stage voice)* Senator Thurmond?

SENATOR: Thank you, Mister Chairman. *(Pause)* Judge Marshall, in view of the fact that your law practice, for many years, before you came with the Federal Government, was concerned with the 13th and 14th amendments, primarily, I would like to ask you some questions in your area of expertise. *(Pause)* Do you know who drafted the 13th amendment?

MARSHALL: No, sir. I don't remember. I have looked it up time after time.

SENATOR: What kind of legislation would, in your estimation, be forbidden by the provision against involuntary servitude?

MARSHALL: I don't know.

SENATOR: Do you believe that the Civil Rights Act of 1866 was constitutional before the ratification of the 14th amendment?

MARSHALL: I am in the middle on that. I researched that when the school cases were up, and I consider it unimportant because the amendment was adopted and they were reenacted. But there was an argument made that—that your statement was true. It was made on the floor of the Congress.

SENATOR: To what extent was the constitutionality of this act supported by reference to the privileges and immunities clause of the article IV, section 2 of the Constitution?

MARSHALL: It was argued.

SENATOR: I didn't catch your answer.

MARSHALL: It was so argued on the floors of Congress.

SENATOR: What theories were then current in
the Republican Party which gave support to the
position that the Civil Rights Act of 1866 could be
constitutionally passed by Congress? *(Pause)* Of what
significance do you believe it is that in deciding the
constitutional basis of the Civil Rights Act of 1866,
Congress copied the enforcement provisions from the
fugitive slave law of 1850?

MARSHALL: *(Patience waning)* Senator, I just don't
remember those debates, which were very voluminous,
and I have not looked at them and have not researched
that point since 1953.

SENATOR: What constitutional difficulties did
Representative John Bingham of Ohio see in
congressional enforcement of article IV, section 2
through the necessary and proper clause of article I,
section 8?

MARSHALL: I don't understand the question.

SENATOR: What constitutional difficulties did
Representative John Bingham of Ohio see in
congressional enforcement of article IV, section 2
through the necessary and proper clause of article I,
section 8?

MARSHALL: I don't see that any...

ROBERT KENNEDY:*(Off stage voice)* I really am confused
as to what actually you are driving at...

SENATOR: Well, Senator Kennedy, I repeated the
question twice.p

ROBERT KENNEDY: Maybe there was some other way
that you could arrive at it?

SENATOR: I don't think I can make it any plainer,
if you know the answer.

ROBERT KENNEDY: I see.

SENATOR: It is just a question of whether you know the answer.

ROBERT KENNEDY: I see. Could you tell us how the solicitor is...

SENATOR: Well, I could tell you that article IV, section 2, *did not set forth the powers vested in the United States. That's the answer!*

ROBERT KENNEDY: *(Ironic)* That's the answer. I see.

(Unchecked laughter is heard in the hearing. Lights indicate a brief passage of time.)

SENATOR: On March 8, 1850, Senator Andrew P Butler, a South Carolina Democrat and a senate colleague of John C Calhoun, stated and I quote:
"A free man of color in South Carolina is not regarded as a citizen by her laws but he has high civil rights. His person and property are protected by law, and he can acquire property, and can claim the protection of the laws for their protection... but they are persons recognized by law, and protected by law."
Now, do you believe this passage shows that the State of South Carolina, while a slave State, was the national leader in giving "civil rights" and "protection of the laws" to colored people, or does it show that these terms had a different meaning a century ago?

MARSHALL: *(Understated irony)* Well, I don't agree that at that time South Carolina was the leader in giving Negroes their rights.

(SENATOR lets out an audible sigh.)

(Lights indicate once again a passage of time.)

SENATOR: Mister Chairman, that is all. I wish to thank the Chairman. Thank you, Judge Marshall.

MARSHALL: Thank you.

CHAIRMAN: You were a judge of the U S Court of Appeals for the Second Circuit?

MARSHALL: Yes, sir.

CHAIRMAN: Did you write a dissenting opinion in the case of *People of New York v. Galamison, 342 F. 2d?*

MARSHALL: Yes, sir.

CHAIRMAN: Page 255?

MARSHALL: Yes, sir.

CHAIRMAN: In that opinion did you make the following statement found at page 279:
"First, peaceful protest, speech and petition, is a form of self-help Not unknown during the era of Reconstruction when Section 1443 (2) was forged?"

MARSHALL: I think so. I don't have the opinion before me, Mr. Chairman.

CHAIRMAN: Did you cite a book as authority?

MARSHALL: I don't remember the book.

CHAIRMAN: By a man named Aptheker, *A Documentary History of the Negro People in the United States?*

MARSHALL: I think I did.

CHAIRMAN: Well, now, of course, *I don't want to leave the impression that you have ever been a Communist or anything like that,* but did you know that at the time you cited this work the author of that book, Herbert Aptheker, had been for many years an avowed Communist and was the leading Communist theoretician in the United States?

MARSHALL: I positively did not know that.

CHAIRMAN: In fact, if you had known that, would you have cited him as an authority?

MARSHALL: I certainly would not...

CHAIRMAN: *(Rudely interrupting)* Well, do you think...

MARSHALL: *(Concluding)* Have done it!

CHAIRMAN: Are you prejudiced against white people in the South?

MARSHALL: *(Momentarily apalled by the question)* Not at all. I was brought up, what I would say way up South in Baltimore. And I worked for white people all my life until I got to college. And from there most of my practice, of course, was in the South, and I don't know, with the possible exception of one person that I was against in the South, that I have any feeling about them.

(End of scene)

Scene Fourteen

(LEZA closes the Congressional book.)

LEZA: Despite an eleven day delay sparked by Eastland, Lyndon Johnson pushed things to a conclusion. On August third, the Committee cast their votes—eleven to five recommending Marshall's confirmation. The full Senate's vote was postponed until the end of August. Strom Thurmond and a few other Southern senators initiated a mini-filibuster to block Marshall. *(Pause)* When the filibuster ended, the Senate went sixty-nine to eleven approving Marshall for his seat on the Supreme Court. The first black man to claim that honor. The President was successful in asking twenty senators to avoid voting - knowing these were southerners at risk for reelection. *(Pause)* The long ordeal was over for Marshall and his family. And on October seventh, 1967 Marshall—now the ninety-sixth Associate Justice of the Supreme Court—privately took the judicial oath in the chambers of justice Hugo Black. *(Segue)* That following

October in Justice Hugo Black's chambers among a very intimate gathering...

(End of scene)

Scene Fifteen

(Justice BLACK's *chambers with* MARSHALL *and* BLACK *in robes. Bible is at hand. October 1967)*

BLACK: Raise your right hand and repeat after me... *(Pause)* "I, Thurgood Marshall...

MARSHALL: I, Thurgood Marshall...

BLACK: ...do solemnly swear

MARSHALL: ...do solemnly swear

BLACK: ...that I will administer Justice without respect...

MARSHALL: ...that I will administer Justice without respect... *(Completes the oath)* ...to persons, and do equal right to the poor and to the rich, and that I will faithfully and impartially discharge and perform all the duties incumbent on me as Associate Justice of Supreme Court of the United States according to the best of my abilities and understanding, agreeably to the Constitution and laws of the United States. *(Pause)* So Help Me God.

(End of scene)

Scene Sixteen

*(*MARSHALL's *one hundred year birthday, and we see a very young* ESSIE MAE *come into the scene like an apparition. She pushes* MARSHALL *slowly in a wheelchair. Washington, DC. 2002)*

LEZA: Senator Thurmond married a second time in 1968 to Nancy Janice Moore—a former "Miss South Carolina 1966" beauty queen. He was nearly three times her age. He fathered four children with her—the last child came in 1976 when the senator was seventy-three years old. *(Pause.* LEZA *focuses on* ESSIE MAE*)* December 5, 2002, just after two P M, two aides helped Senator Thurmond through a fawning crowd in the Dirksen Senate Office Building. About five hundred guests came to salute the oldest and longest-presiding senator in American history, a man who became one hundred years old, a Southerner seen as an unforgettable living monument to the Capitol. The Air Force christened its hundredth C-17 cargo plane "Spirit of Strom Thurmond. *(Pause)* A strong showing of members from the House and the Senate were at the Dirksen Building, including four Supreme Court justices—enjoying chocolate-covered strawberries and bowls of banana and butter pecan ice cream. They stood in an absurdly long receiving line to greet the centenarian, who was displayed on a small rake by the podium.

(ESSIE MAE *takes a samll plate of cake and begins to feed the* SENATOR.*)*

ESSIE MAE: Do you like the dessert?

SENATOR: I like the butter pecan, yes. *(Pause. Studying her face lovingly)* You look so much younger and so elegant. Is that a new hat?

ESSIE MAE: *(She nods. It is the same hat as in Scene One.)* All your friends are here.

SENATOR: Are they here?

ESSIE MAE: All too many, sir. This is a very big event.

SENATOR: Can they see you?

ESSIE MAE: No.

SENATOR: Are you sure?

ESSIE MAE: Happy birthday, Daddy. (*She kisses him on the forehead and moves away.*)

LEZA: The Senator seemed at times in a fog and then sharply alert. His eyes were tearing frequently. At three P M precisely, the room quieted for a round of sincere tributes and roasting jokes. Among the speakers were Senator Trent Lott, the majority leader, who stated that his eighty-nine year old mother *still* has a crush on Strom. Lott boasted that his home state of Mississippi had supported Thurmond's Dixiecrat 1948 presidency campaign and that—"if the rest of the country had followed our lead we wouldn't have had all these problems over all these years." (*Pause*) The political fallout was great for Trent Lott. A good many people in the media faulted Lott for speaking code about the nostalgia for racial segregation and Lott had to step down from his party's leadership. (*Pause*) The Senator's party culminated in a surprise appearance by an awful Marilyn Monroe impersonator. She sang to Thurmond with a strained rendition of "Happy Birthday, Mister President Pro Tempore" and kissed his wide forehead, leaving a red lipstick mark in the shape of the state of South Carolina.

(*Singing* Happy Birthday, ESSIE MAE *wheels in a one hundred candle cake in front of the* SENATOR *and he is in tears. He reaches for a small microphone.*)

SENATOR: Ladies and gentlemen, I don't know how to thank you. You're beautiful people and I appreciate what you've done for me and may God allow you to live long and enjoy the time."

ESSIE MAE: (*Direct address to the audience*) At which point, the Senator's daughter Julie Thurmond Whitmer stepped to the podium and told the crowd that she was expecting his first *white* grandchild on the *4th of July.*

SENATOR: *(Looking far away, to Julie Thurmond Whitmer)*
I knew you'd give me exactly what I wanted

*(The sound of a crowd applauding him and perhaps
celebration music.)*

(End of scene)

EPILOGUE

(LEZA addressing ESSIE MAE's house in Los Angeles)

LEZA: Thurgood Marshall and Strom Thurmond.
Two profoundly different political figures. They evoke
the entire terrain of American race relations over the
last sixty years. Perhaps their ghosts know that Jim
Crow may not be dead after all. *(Pause)* The percentage
of blacks in majority white Southern schools, which
peaked in 1988 at forty-three percent, had dropped to
thirty-one percent by 2000 On one hand, our country
has made tremendous progress in the last fifty years of
race relations. On the other hand, because of economics
and class exclusivity we are seeing disturbing rollbacks
to Supreme Court's victory over Jim Crow. *(Pause)*
I'm standing outside Essie-Mae's house in Los Angeles.
This is an ordinary home blending in with the many
other homes on either side of the street. I know
Essie-Mae lives here. I want to knock very loud and
forcefully on her front door. There's a surge of anger
welling up inside me. I expect her to come to the door.
I owe it to her to know how I feel. My emotions should
spill into hers. My tears are real and I can taste the salt..
I know that she deserves privacy, yet I must ask her one
very direct question. *(Pause)* Mrs Washington-Williams,
may I please call you Essie-Mae? Do you remember me
at all? Of course you do. Of course. Essie-Mae is such
a beautiful name. My name is Leza Violet, but no one
uses my middle name any more. Essie-Mae, please tell

me how your children convinced you to talk in public about your natural white, famous father of the old South? Essie-Mae, is it true that your son Ronald Williams, claims that he was a registered Republican before Strom Thurmond was? Essie-Mae, please look me in the eyes. Please remember something about me. I so need to talk to you. *(Pause)* I'm standing outside Essie-Mae's house in Los Angeles. I am ninety-nine percent certain that this is her home. Once she opens the door, I imagine the many ways she plans to answer my question . She declares her basic right to privacy. She tells me that her children had asked her to do this, decades ago. She explains that she dearly loved and respected Senator Strom Thurmond. She cries discreetly and looks away. She shows me a letter that she had planned to release after her death. She bites her lip and says that she has no explanation whatsoever. She smiles softly, a warm grandmother's smile, and she says that the nation is ready to hear the news. There are no slaves and nor mistresses left in America. There is only one toilet and only one water fountain and only one classroom for all of America's children. The nation has waited long to heal. *(Pause)* I'm standing outside Essie-Mae's house in Los Angeles. A bus goes by. Essie-Mae could have been another Rosa Parks.

END OF PLAY

www.ingramcontent.com/pod-product-compliance
Lightning Source LLC
Chambersburg PA
CBHW070031110426
42741CB00035B/2719